Empowering Skulls :
A Journey of Strength,
Mindfulness, and Positivity

Lex, Max & Belle

Let your passions fuel your journey

Let your creativity flow like a river

Uncover the hidden potential within you

Dare to dream big and achieve greatness

Embrace the rhythm
of life and dance
to your own beat

Rhythmic Dance Skull

Believe in the power of your own strength

Inner Strength Skull

Love and accept
yourself
unconditionally

Cherish the gift of friendship and connection

Bonded Souls Skull

Transform your fears into courage

Every breath you take is an opportunity for gratitude

Grateful Breath Skull

Let your positive energy light up the world

Radiant Energy Skull

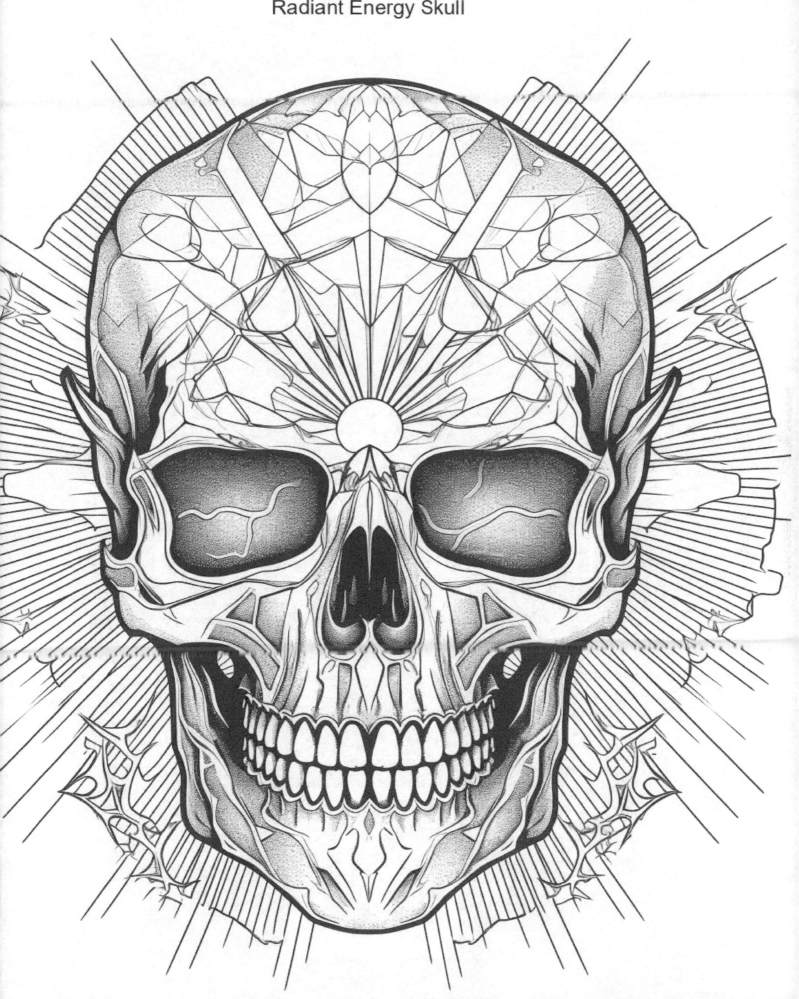

Embrace the wisdom that comes with age

Choose to see the beauty in every challenge

Cultivate a mindset of abundance and prosperity

You are the author
of your own story

Celebrate the unique song of your soul

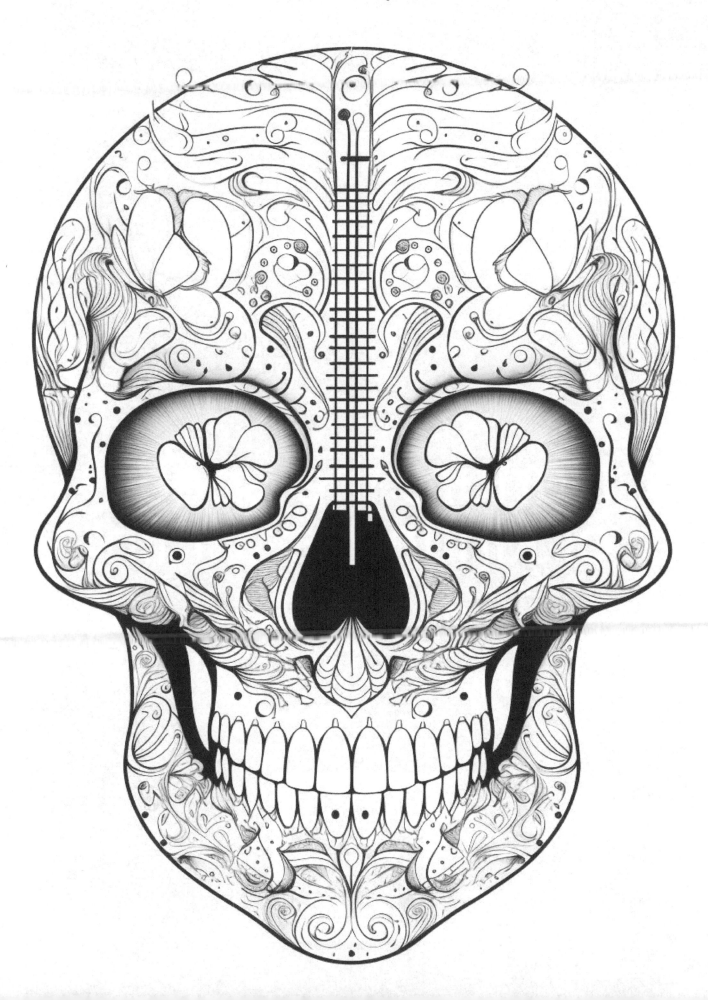

Soulful Melody Skull

Nurture the seeds of kindness within you

Recognize the power of resilience in times of adversity

Resilient Phoenix Skull

Be the change you wish to see in the world

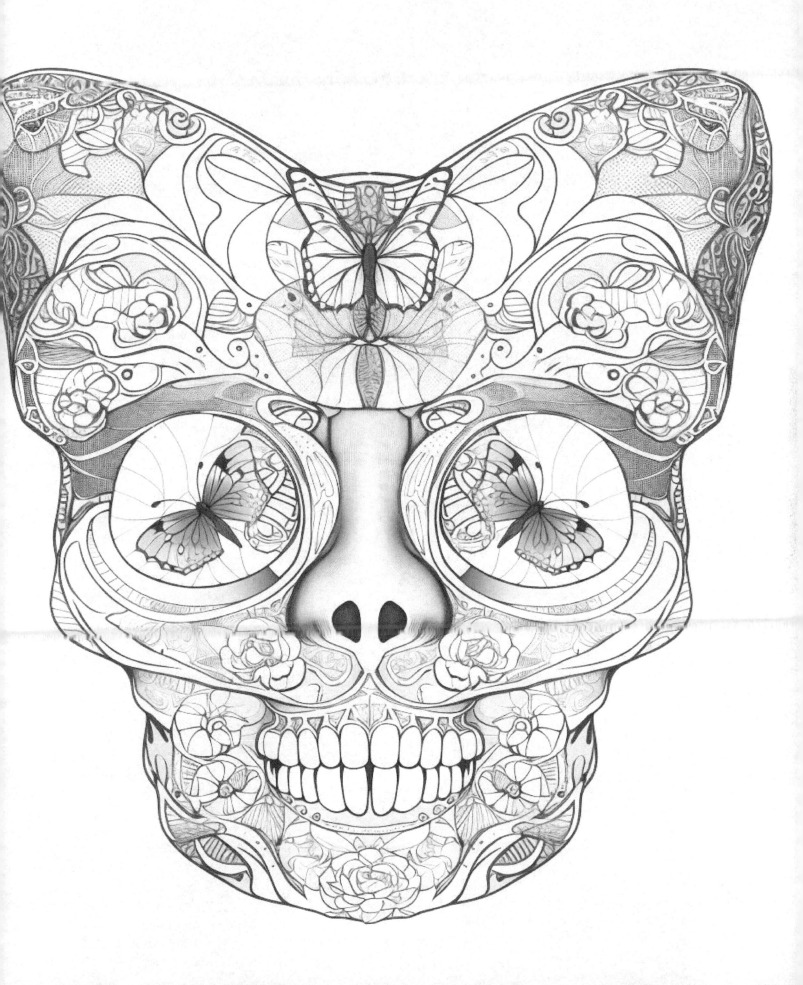

Metamorphic Change Skull

Embrace the support of your loved ones

Trust in the journey and let go of expectations

Explore the depths of your own soul

Find balance and harmony in all aspects of life

Keep moving forward, one step at a time

Discover the hidden treasures within you

Awaken to the beauty of the world around you

Take time to appreciate the small wonders of life

Cultivate a spirit of adventure and curiosity

Laugh often and embrace the joy in life

Joyful Laughter Skull

Dream without limits and manifest your desires

Embrace the healing power of nature

Healing Nature Skull

Cultivate inner peace and tranquility

Embrace your uniqueness and let your light shine

Honor your roots and celebrate your heritage

Appreciate the interconnectedness of all living things

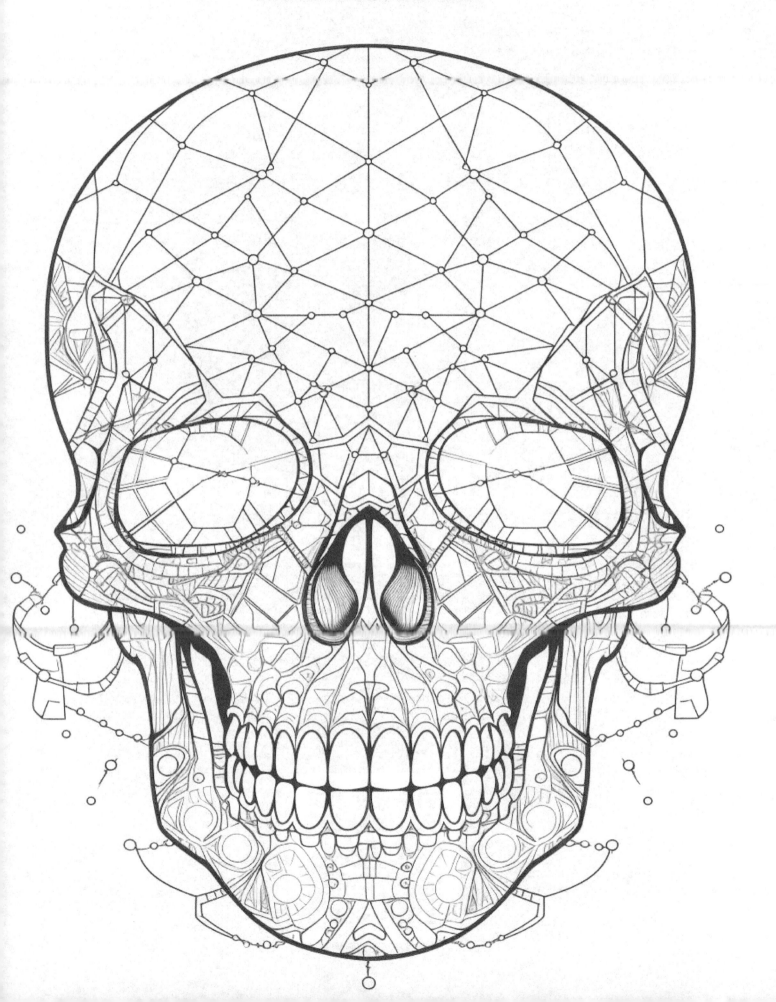

Let the winds of change guide your sails

Embrace your inner warrior and face your fears

Fearless Warrior Skull

Nurture the creative spirit within you

Creative Blossom Skull

Embrace the transformative power of love

Honor the cycles of life and the passage of time

Cycles of Time Skull

Find the courage to break free from limitations

Seek inner wisdom through self-reflection

Be a beacon of hope in times of darkness

Hopeful Beacon Skull

Embrace your vulnerability and find strength in it

Nurture your mind, body, and spirit with care

Celebrate the triumphs and learn from the challenges

Embrace the magic of the present moment

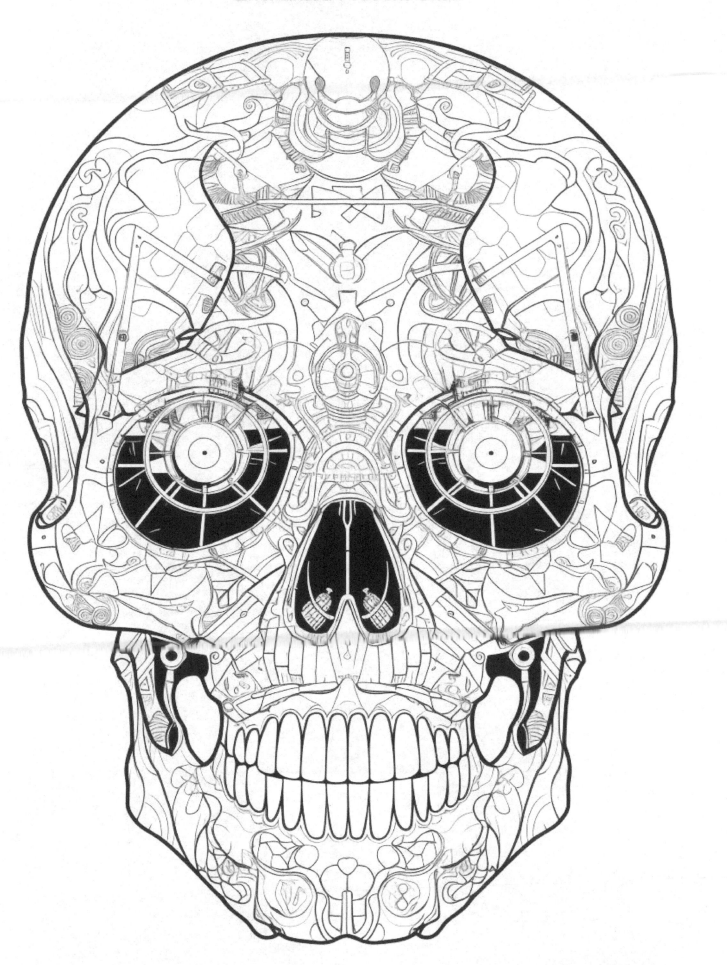

Find solace in the beauty of solitude

Choose happiness and let it fill your soul

Embrace the journey of self-discovery

Believe in your ability to create a better world

Reconnect with the wisdom of your ancestors

Including additional designs on line

www.g5cloud.com/lexmaxbelle-books/empowering-skulls/additional-designs-en.pdf

Thank you !

More books on

www.g5cloud.com/lexmaxbelle

Follow us

www.amazon.com/author/lexmaxbelle

Contact us

lexmaxbelle@g5cloud.com

Made in the USA
Las Vegas, NV
29 May 2023

72692464R00059